T0070026

ORIGINAL SQUISHMALLOWS ™

AUTHENTIC PRODUCT

Squishmallows: The Official Collector's Guide
©2022 Kelly Toys Holdings, LLC. All rights reserved.
Squishmallow and Squishmallows are trademarks of Kelly Toys Holdings, LLC.
Additional images supplied by Shutterstock.

All rights reserved. Printed in Canada. No part of this publication may be reproduced,
stored in a retrieval system, or transmitted, in any form or by any means, electronic, mechanical,
photocopying, recording or otherwise, without the prior permission of the publisher and copyright owner.
For information address HarperCollins Children's Books, a division of HarperCollins Publishers,
195 Broadway, New York, NY 10007.
www.harpercollinschildrens.com

Stay safe online. HarperCollins Publishers is not responsible for content hosted by third parties.

ISBN 978-0-06-321965-6

23 24 25 26 PC/TC 10 9 8 7 6 5 4 3
❖
Originally published in Great Britain by Farshore, 2022

AUTHENTIC PRODUCT

ORIGINAL SQUISHMALLOWS™

THE OFFICIAL COLLECTOR'S GUIDE

HARPER

An Imprint of HarperCollins*Publishers*

WELCOME TO THE WORLD OF ORIGINAL SQUISHMALLOWS ™

...the squishiest, friendliest, most colorful place of all!

Get the lowdown on the Squishmallows' squads and squishdates, and discover epic facts— hundreds of Squishmallows are waiting to meet you, from **Aimee** to **Zeke**!

Jam-packed with **250** of your favorite **Squishmallows**, this **Official Collectors' Guide** is the one-stop handbook for all 'Mallows fans!

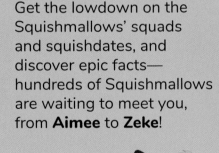

CONTENTS

TIME TO CELEBRATE!

100 MILLION SQUISHMALLOWS SOLD BY 2021

... That's **100 million** thrilling Squishmallows hunts, **100 million** little victory dances, and **100 million** smiles! This mega milestone could not have been reached without each and every one of you, **our favorite squad of all!**

Because of **YOU**, the Squishmallows Squad has grown all across the globe. We think that's pretty amazing! Almost as amazing as you! So, let us say **thank you— 100 million times** over!

To commemorate this momentous 100-millionth milestone in true Squishmallows style, **100 Select Series** Hans toys were released into the wild! Were you one of the lucky few able to add Golden Hans or Hans with Gold Details to your collection?

Assemble your Squishmallows squad and let's celebrate!

CAM
the Calico Cat

WOW! fact
Did you know that Cam's tricolor coat makes him a calico cat?

RARITY RATINGS: REVEALED!

While many 'Mallows can be commonly found, some carry a special seal on their tags. But what do they mean and how hard are these Squishmallows to track down? Here's a handy guide to help you on your next squish hunt!

RARE

Want to find rare Squishmallows to add to your squad? Hunt for the shiny silver tag! The special silver-foiled **Rare** Squishmallows tag means only 75,000 of these 'Mallows exist in the whole world! Get them while they last!

ULTRA RARE

Have you found a 'Mallow with a golden tag? Congrats— you've tracked down one of the **Ultra Rare** Squishmallows! Only 50,000 of these **Ultra Rare** Squishmallows exist worldwide, and only at select retailers. Lucky you!

SPECIAL EDITION

Keep your eyes peeled for the holographic Squishmallows tag. These **Special Edition** 'Mallows are extremely rare with 20,000 maximum of them out in the wild! A limited amount of these super-special Squishmallows are released before they're retired, so grab them while you can!

SELECT SERIES

With up to 10,000 'Mallows released on Squishmallows.com, **Select Series** are some of the rarest Squishmallows of all! A very limited amount of new **Select Series** Squishmallows are released each month, so look for the elusive black tag. Once they're gone, they're gone!

FOUNDER'S EDITION

The **Founder's Edition** tag is given to some seriously rare Squishmallows! Want one? Well you won't meet these 'Mallows in the wild! Find a rare Founder's Redemption Card hidden in a select few decks of Squishmallows Series 1 Trading Cards, then use the code to redeem a special **Founder's Edition** 'Mallow! Good luck!

CHECK-IN SERIES

Adventure calls! Squishmallows with a purple tag are part of the **Check-In Series**. These 'Mallows can only be found at select locations, so get exploring.

If you've not found any of the six special seals yet, keep hunting—those elusive Squishmallows often pop up when you least expect it!

SQUISHMALLOWS IN NUMBERS

Ever tried to figure out just why Squishmallows are #1? It's a numbers game!

1000+
Squishmallows to collect

1

40+
Countries where you can buy Squishmallows

12
Different squads featured in this guide

The first of the Squishmallows —Cam the Calico Cat

Only **500**
16" Jack plush toys were ever produced

11

The number of different sizes Squishmallows have been made in ... so far

999

Raisy's collector number

2

SELECT
Squishmallows in this book

2017

The year the first Squishmallows were born!

100 MILLION

Squishmallows toys sold by November 2021!

Almost **100** figurines in Chet's collection

50+

Countries that Xandra has visited

15

Introducing ...

WINSTON

the Teal Owl

WOW! fact

Winston's freshly baked cupcakes include a secret ingredient—love!

SQUAD UP!

Each 'Mallow belongs to a special squad that reflects their interests, hobbies, aspirations, emotions, or even their name! Which squad is your favorite?

CLASSIC

The awesome **Classic Squad** includes the original and most iconic Squishmallows from the first one thousand created! Each has its own unique and fun personality and will make a great addition to any collection.

COSTUME

If there is one thing 'Mallows love, it's playing dress-up. The **Costume Squad** is always switching it up with different silly and unexpected outfits so they never get bored!

18

FANTASY

With the **Fantasy Squad**, you never know just who you'll meet. Unicorns, rainbow owls, and mystical dragons—anything is possible in this imaginative squad!

FOOD

Sweet or savory, this yummy squad has something for everyone. From tacos to s'mores, 'Mallows in the **Food Squad** are as cute as they are delicious.

NATURE

Venture outside to find the **Nature Squad**, bursting with leafy succulents, happy cacti, colorful flowers, and tons of other earthy 'Mallows! They're a breath of fresh air, and sure to brighten up any collection!

BUDDY

The **Buddy Squad** is a lively and playful group of 'Mallows. They're quick to join a game of fetch, chase a ball of yarn, or even splash around in a fishbowl. Two things they'll never turn down—belly rubs and treats!

PREHISTORIC

The **Prehistoric Squad** is a rag-tag team of Dinos all the way from the Mesozoic era. Don't be fooled by their horns, scraggly fur, and scales, they're super friendly and are always ready for cuddles!

SEALIFE

Beneath the water's surface is a flourishing **Sealife Squad**. These marine 'Mallows make their homes in the blue ocean, among colorful coral reefs, floating green kelp beds, and sparkling tide pools.

SEASONAL

This **Seasonal Squad** is full of festive 'Mallows. Whether you're feeling sweet or spooky, this squad has something for every time of the year.

SELECT

The **Select Squad** is the rarest of the rare. Blink and you might miss these limited-edition 'Mallows!

SPACE

The **Space Squad** is a far-out collection of everything under the sun. This intergalactic crew is made up of astronauts, aliens, and distant planets, and more, all ready to explore the farthest reaches of the galaxy.

WILDLIFE

Find the **Wildlife Squad** roaming in deeply wooded forests, lush jungles, and desert landscapes. From birds to bison to butterflies, this squad of 'Mallows was born wild and free.

Look out for more **squads** coming soon!

21

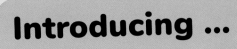

Introducing ...

LOLA

the **Tie-Dye Unicorn**

WOW! fact

Want to know how Lola stays so calm and happy? Spa treatments, at least once a week!

SQUISH HUNTING

Do you remember your very first squish hunt? Or that time you hit the jackpot and added that super-rare 'Mallow to your squad? Here's who you told us you loved to track down!

Squish hunters in the US showed these 'Mallows the love! Meet **Malcolm**, **Archie, Benny**, and **Connor**!

From the US to the UK, **Wendy** is a firm favorite of Squish hunters! Has she hopped into your squad yet?

The **Sealife Squad** was once voted #1 by fans in a social media poll! How do you rate this squad?

HAPPY HUNTING!

SQUISH CROSS!

Here's a puzzle that will bring cheer to all Squishmallows collectors! Read the clues to help you fill in the answers in the crossword.

DOWN

1. An adventurous fox who loves travel and yoga. (4)

2. The prickly species to which happy Hans belongs. (8)

4. Lola's squad is known simply as this. (7)

7. Gordon, Sheldon, and Starla are all members of this squad. (7)

9. Last but not least, the final guy in the Meet the 'Mallows section. (4)

ACROSS

3. A paw-some pug who's royally named. (6)

5. The #1 'Mallow in the collection! (3)

6. This owl loves to cook up a storm! (7)

8. The color of a sleek meowing 'Mallow. (5)

10. 'Mallows with black tags are part of this exclusive series. (6)

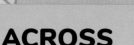

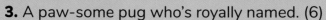

TOO TRICKY? FLIP TO THE *MEET THE 'MALLOWS!* PAGES TO LOOK FOR CLUES.

Answers are on page 192

27

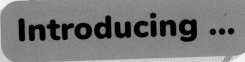

HANS

the Hedgehog

**WOW!
fact**

Hans's favorite way
to watch movies is
in 3D. Don't forget
the popcorn!

MEET THE 'MALLOWS!

The next section gives you the stats and facts that every Squishmallows collector needs to build their squad. You'll discover:

The name of the Squishmallow.

Which squad it belongs to.

Its squishdate—the date when a Squishmallow was given its name.

Some profiles mention 'Mallows that couldn't be squished into this book! Meet them at Squishmallows.com.

Its collector number.

A brief bio that explains what makes each and every 'Mallow unique!

CHET

> **Squad:** Wildlife
> **Squishdate:** October 25, 2020
> **Collector number:** #633

Bobbleheads and sneakers are two things that **CHET** the iguana loves to collect. He has almost 100 figurines, and a wild story for almost every pair of sneakers—just wait until you hear about his latest pair!

Look out for facts about the original 'Mallows Cam, Winston, Lola, Hans, and Fifi throughout the book!

Check out **Select Series Jack** on page 37!

Now flip the page to meet 250 fun-loving Squishmallows!

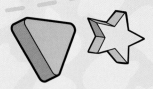

CAM

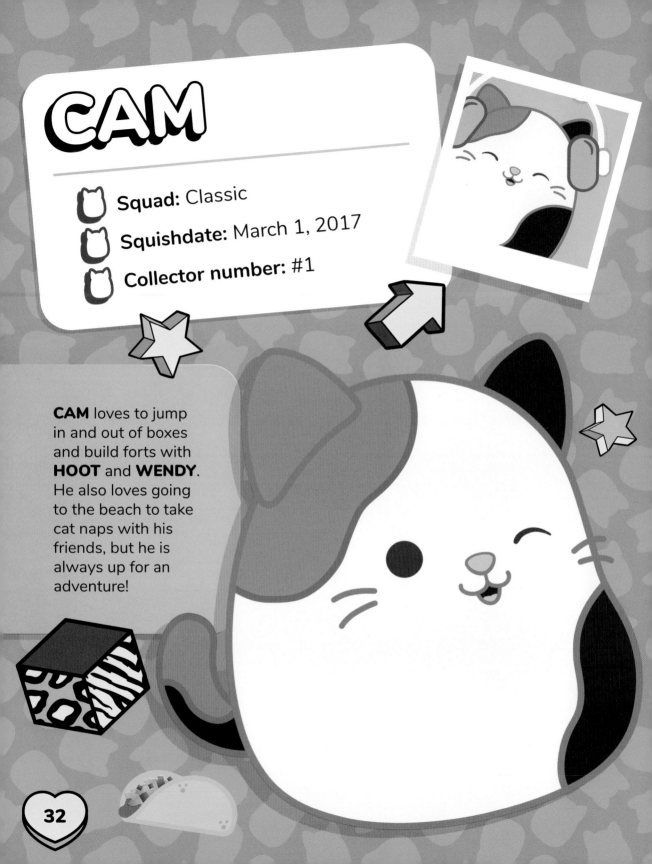

- **Squad:** Classic
- **Squishdate:** March 1, 2017
- **Collector number:** #1

CAM loves to jump in and out of boxes and build forts with **HOOT** and **WENDY**. He also loves going to the beach to take cat naps with his friends, but he is always up for an adventure!

WINSTON

- **Squad:** Classic
- **Squishdate:** March 1, 2018
- **Collector number:** #92

WINSTON the owl is an aspiring chef who takes his cooking creativity to the next level. His friends inspire his latest culinary delights, and he's always ready to whip up his famous mac 'n' cheese.

33

LOLA

Squad: Classic

Squishdate: December 1, 2017

Collector number: #84

Unicorn **LOLA** loves the color pink, and watching movies with her friends. She wants to be an actress when she grows up. **LOLA** loves to visit new places and dreams of traveling the world while she makes movies.

HANS

- **Squad:** Classic
- **Squishdate:** March 1, 2017
- **Collector number:** #2

Two special edition **HANS** Squishmallows were released as part of the 100 millionth sales celebrations!

Hedgehog **HANS** has seen every movie ever! His favorite snack is popcorn with chocolate-covered raisins, because when it comes to food, he's willing to try everything. **HANS** loves having adventures.

35

FIFI

 Squad: Classic

Squishdate: March 17, 2017

Collector number: #5

FIFI is your girl if you like to go on adventures! She's traveled to the Arctic, to the mountains, and is ready to go on her next trip with you. This fox has a vibrant personality and is quite the little firecracker. She channels her energy through yoga, and is working on getting her yoga teacher certificate!

JACK

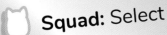
Squad: Select

Squishdate: September 1, 2020

Collector number: #500

500

JACK is the strong, silent type, but this cat is always there when you need him. He's not afraid to speak up for himself or his friends. He can be a little feisty, but he loves to cuddle. **JACK** loves giving back and thinks we should always lend a helping paw.

FUN FACT
Super-popular **JACK** sold out in 2 hours when released online!

37

AIMEE

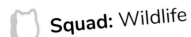

- Squad: Wildlife
- Squishdate: July 1, 2018
- Collector number: #127

This chick has got quite the résumé! From clubs and competitions to concerts and more, **AIMEE** is a busy bee, both on and off the stage. In her spare time, she plans events that she isn't even a part of and hopes to be in charge of red-carpet events someday.

ANASTASIA

- **Squad:** Sealife
- **Squishdate:** September 16, 2020
- **Collector number:** #562

If you need some help starting a project, **ANASTASIA** is the axolotl for you! She is a planner and likes to be prepared for everything—**ANASTASIA** keeps track of her ideas by writing lists. How can she assist you?

ANDRES

- **Squad:** Buddy
- **Squishdate:** July 10, 2019
- **Collector number:** #269

ANDRES is a very silly 'Mallow! He loves practical jokes and hearing people laugh. This sheepdog wants to be a comedian when he grows up—do you know any good jokes that he could tell?

ANGIE

- **Squad:** Buddy
- **Squishdate:** July 10, 2019
- **Collector number:** #270

ANGIE adores a good fiesta—she loves going to parties and events as much as she enjoys hosting them. When **ANGIE** hosts, she makes specially themed food and drinks for her friends. Want to know some of this Shiba Inu's favorite things to make? Guacamole, peanut butter brownies, and samosas!

ARCHER

Squad: Wildlife

Squishdate: December 19, 2020

Collector number: #750

ARCHER dreams of being a black belt, but there's just one problem—he isn't very athletic! This alligator always tries his best for his sensei and knows he will get better with time. Would you mind practicing with him?

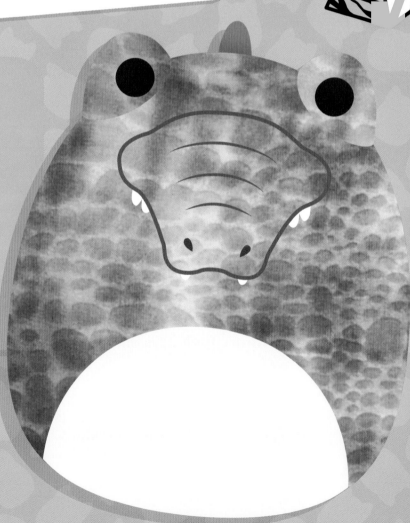

42

ARCHIE

Squad: Sealife

Squishdate: July 18, 2019

Collector number: #275

Have you met axolotl **ARCHIE**? This 'Mallow has a special talent—he communicates with his hands using Squishmallows Sign! He also loves playing soccer. One day he might play in the 'Mallows Cup!

ASHLEY

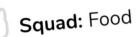

- **Squad:** Food
- **Squishdate:** September 27, 2019
- **Collector number:** #334

Apple **ASHLEY** loves table tennis—one day she wants to be part of the world's best table tennis team! For now, she practices with her friends and hosts backyard tournaments. You can help her keep score!

AUSTIN

- **Squad:** Food
- **Squishdate:** September 27, 2019
- **Collector number:** #330

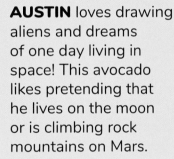

AUSTIN loves drawing aliens and dreams of one day living in space! This avocado likes pretending that he lives on the moon or is climbing rock mountains on Mars. AUSTIN became obsessed with outer space in school after reading a book about aliens. Will you help him plan his next space adventure?

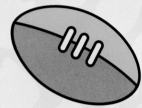

AVERY

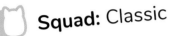

Squad: Classic

Squishdate: April 15, 2019

Collector number: #216

Don't let his size fool you, **AVERY** the duck is a skilled left-winger for the 'Mallows rugby team. One day, he wants to be a coach! His whole family comes to watch, bringing Popsicles to celebrate once the game is over.

AZIZA

- **Squad:** Sealife
- **Squishdate:** December 23, 2020
- **Collector number:** #761

AZIZA the stingray is like a typical teen. Sarcasm, sleeping in, and being silly are just a few of her favorite things. If you need a second opinion or a new topic to debate, **AZIZA** is the 'Mallow for you!

BABS

Squad: Wildlife

Squishdate: September 25, 2020

Collector number: #467

Blue jay **BABS** loves superheroes, sci-fi, and has even created her own superhero, Captain Blueberry— a regular bird by day who solves crimes by night. Now **BABS** just needs to invent a sidekick. What should she call them?

48

BELLA

- **Squad:** Wildlife
- **Squishdate:** November 10, 2017
- **Collector number:** #66

BELLA has a fine-tuned spider sense. She's a palm reader and a gifted magician. As the darkness creeps in, she goes from a regular 'Mallow to a girl with tricks up her sleeves.

BENNY

- **Squad:** Fantasy
- **Squishdate:** March 11, 2020
- **Collector number:** #433

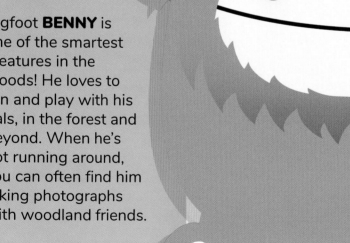

Bigfoot **BENNY** is one of the smartest creatures in the woods! He loves to run and play with his pals, in the forest and beyond. When he's not running around, you can often find him taking photographs with woodland friends.

BERNARDO

 Squad: Food

 Squishdate: November 20, 2020

Collector number: #691

If you want a spicy surprise, be sure to catch burrito **BERNARDO** on the baby grand piano every Friday night. He only sings in Spanish. By the time you leave, you might be able to sing in Spanish too!

BERNICE

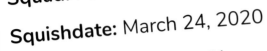

 Squad: Food

 Squishdate: March 24, 2020

 Collector number: #451

Blissful, bubbly, and bright. Three words to describe the best boba tea you'll meet! **BERNICE** is sweet, but not too sweet. She always lends a helping hand to her friends.

BERNIE

- **Squad:** Classic
- **Squishdate:** February 5, 2019
- **Collector number:** #188

BERNIE loves the mountains and helping other people more than anything else in the world. His dream is to work in emergency response and assist with mountain rescues. When **BERNIE**'s not saving lives, you will find the Saint Bernard enjoying the snowy weather. He keeps himself entertained by romping, rolling, and pulling his friends on sleds!

BETHANY

- **Squad:** Fantasy
- **Squishdate:** October 6, 2020
- **Collector number:** #611

BETHANY's favorite meal is breakfast, but she also loves the fresh biscuits her mom makes every Friday night for dinner. This cute koala likes helping in the garden, looking after the yummy berries that her mom uses for jam-making.

BLAKE

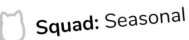

- **Squad:** Seasonal
- **Squishdate:** October 20, 2020
- **Collector number:** #52-4

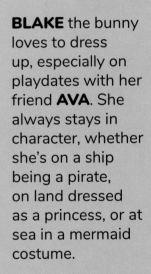

BLAKE the bunny loves to dress up, especially on playdates with her friend **AVA**. She always stays in character, whether she's on a ship being a pirate, on land dressed as a princess, or at sea in a mermaid costume.

BLANCA

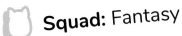

Squad: Fantasy

Squishdate: September 5, 2019

Collector number: #305

Even though she's a rainbow kangaroo, **BLANCA**'s favorite color is black. She loves to draw and paint in black and white, and even designs her own artsy Easter baskets for her friends.

BLAZE

- **Squad:** Seasonal
- **Squishdate:** February 20, 2020
- **Collector number:** #415

Ready for a haunted house extraordinaire? Monster **BLAZE** is the 'Mallow for you! He makes sure that every spiderweb, headless horsemallow, and creepy cauldron are in the right place for the Halloween Mansion.

BRENDA

Squad: Wildlife

Squishdate: March 13, 2019

Collector number: #206

Butterfly **BRENDA** loves to be outside, enjoying the sun! She has a green thumb, and sells flowers from her garden at the farmers market every week. Her favorite flowers are marigolds and phlox.

BRINA

- **Squad:** Fantasy
- **Squishdate:** March 11, 2020
- **Collector number:** #432

Say hi to **BRINA** the Bigfoot. This confident little creature likes going on new adventures. **BRINA**'s favorite season is winter, because her favorite sport is snowboarding. She waits all year to participate in the local snowboarding competition.

BRISBY

Squad: Classic

Squishdate: April 15, 2019

Collector number: #213

"Home on the Range" is one of **BRISBY** the horse's favorite songs—he loves spending time on the ranch with his family. If you get the chance, you should join him camping in the mountains, where he whips up some delicious s'mores.

BROCK

- **Squad:** Buddy
- **Squishdate:** September 2, 2018
- **Collector number:** #134

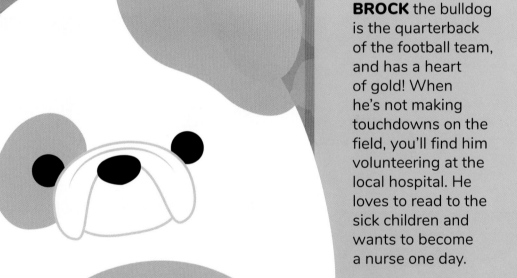

BROCK the bulldog is the quarterback of the football team, and has a heart of gold! When he's not making touchdowns on the field, you'll find him volunteering at the local hospital. He loves to read to the sick children and wants to become a nurse one day.

BROOKE

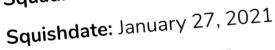

 Squad: Seasonal

Squishdate: January 27, 2021

Collector number: #72-5

BROOKE and her friend **ZELINA** are getting ready for a very special day. Since **BROOKE** the polar bear knows a thing or two about candy, she's helping **ZELINA** paint sugar skulls for Día de los Muertos! Would you like to join in the fun?

BRUCE

- **Squad:** Sealife
- **Squishdate:** October 22, 2018
- **Collector number:** #160

Want to explore the beauty of Alaska? **BRUCE** the seal is your guy! An active kayaker, **BRUCE** leads travelers on amazing river tours, and shows them all of his favorite hidden gems. Get ready for a photo op!

BUZZ

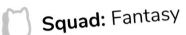
- **Squad:** Fantasy
- **Squishdate:** June 24, 2019
- **Collector number:** #249

If you give a sloth a donut, he's sure to want more! Especially **BUZZ**—the way to this smooth sloth's heart is through his stomach. Another thing about **BUZZ** is that he seems to know EVERYTHING! The buzz on **BUZZ** is that he's the best secret-keeper in town.

CALTON

- **Squad:** Wildlife
- **Squishdate:** April 22, 2021
- **Collector number:** #995

Learn to cook with **CALTON**! He loves food: making everything from lasagna to pot pies. When **CALTON** isn't whipping up delicious food, he's probably taking a quick snooze. What kind of food can this Highland cow show you how to cook?

CAMILO

Squad: Buddy

Squishdate: June 2, 2021

Collector number: #1033

Meet **CAMILO**. This mouse is a musical theater major, whose dream is to be onstage. **CAMILO** has been taking voice, dance, and acting lessons for years, and knows all the words to the big musicals. Do you want to sing and dance with **CAMILO**?

CANNON

- **Squad:** Seasonal
- **Squishdate:** December 10, 2018
- **Collector number:** #179

CANNON is a wellness coach who teaches kids how to make healthy meals. However, this candy corn can't resist a sweet treat during Halloween, so he makes his famous caramel apples for himself and all the trick-or-treaters!

CARL

Squad: Food

Squishdate: March 24, 2020

Collector number: #450

Meet **CARL**. He loves practical jokes and hanging out with his burger bros. When he was just a little 'Mallow patty, he dreamed of one day being the funniest cheeseburger in the pack.

CARLOS

- **Squad:** Sealife
- **Squishdate:** December 16, 2019
- **Collector number:** #387

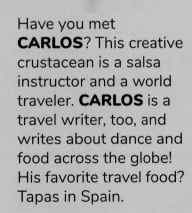

Have you met **CARLOS**? This creative crustacean is a salsa instructor and a world traveler. **CARLOS** is a travel writer, too, and writes about dance and food across the globe! His favorite travel food? Tapas in Spain.

CARMELITA

- **Squad:** Food
- **Squishdate:** November 18, 2020
- **Collector number:** #683

Do you like manga? Then you should check out some of **CARMELITA**'s work. She draws black-and-white manga about school, her life, and adventures with her best friend **CINNAMON**. Don't worry about this s'more spilling any secrets—**CARMELITA** uses code names for any juicy stuff.

CAROL

- **Squad:** Seasonal
- **Squishdate:** March 31, 2020
- **Collector number:** #456

Caroling, cocoa, and cookies are some of Christmas tree **CAROL**'s favorite things. This festive 'Mallow loves the bright and cheery vibe of the holidays, and wishes the world could be that way every day. She sings in an a capella group that visits schools, homes, and hospitals to sing festive tunes all year round.

CAROLEENA

- **Squad:** Food
- **Squishdate:** October 13, 2020
- **Collector number:** #623

Ready for a laugh? **CAROLEENA** is the queen of impressions. Even if you're in a bad mood, this carrot will have you laughing in no time. Her impressions are spot on, and she can stay in character for a long time. Once she made her aunt laugh so hard, she broke a table!

CAZLAN

 Squad: Wildlife

Squishdate: October 29, 2020

Collector number: #636

Did you see that flash of red soaring through the skies? It must be **CAZLAN**! This speedy cardinal loves to zoom about, but when she finally lands, it's time to get her nerd on with her BFF, **BABS**. One day, **CAZLAN** wants to be **BAB**'s sidekick!

CELIA

- **Squad:** Food
- **Squishdate:** November 24, 2020
- **Collector number:** #712

Roller coasters and beach trips are two things that **CELIA** the orange loves to do every summer. She adores going to the amusement park and screams on all her favorite rides. The rides are on the boardwalk, so she can see the ocean just before the drop. Want to tag along next time?

CELINE

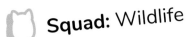

- **Squad:** Wildlife
- **Squishdate:** November 7, 2019
- **Collector number:** #367

You might never meet a sweeter 'Mallow than **CELINE** the chicken—she wants to help everyone she meets. Her aunt works for a nonprofit charity that helps 'Mallows in other parts of the world, and when **CELINE** grows up, she wants to work there too.

CHANEL

- **Squad:** Food
- **Squishdate:** March 24, 2020
- **Collector number:** #455

Meet **CHANEL**. This sweet cinnamon-roll pastry chef loves giving back. In her spare time she volunteers at the local food charity and teaches cake baking and decorating.

CHARITY

- **Squad:** Wildlife
- **Squishdate:** October 11, 2019
- **Collector number:** #348

Guess who just learned how to ride a bike? **CHARITY** did! She has a blue-and-purple bike with streamers on the handlebars. She used to be afraid of falling, but then she got right back up and tried again. Will you go on bike rides with **CHARITY** the chicken?

CHARLIE

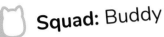 Squad: Buddy

 Squishdate: December 1, 2017

 Collector number: #80

This little terrier is always on the go. **CHARLIE** has had the travel bug since he was little. He has been spotted in some of the finest places in the world. It makes sense, since he aspires to break the news as a future reporter someday!

CHARLIZE

Squad: Buddy

Squishdate: September 7, 2020

Collector number: #523

Meet **CHARLIZE**. She is a professional masseuse and thinks everyone could use a little more self-care. This cockatiel is very strong and loves soothing her fellow 'Mallows whenever they need some TLC. What does she do for her own self-care? A nice weekend to herself in a cabin far, far away.

CHASE

 Squad: Fantasy

Squishdate: July 17, 2019

Collector number: #273

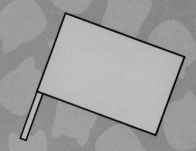

CHASE loves camping, canoes, and capture the flag. Every summer, he goes on a trip with his 'Mallow Squad and they have a blast—last year it was **CHASE** who found the opposing team's flag! If you love the outdoors, then **CHASE** is the cat for you.

CHET

- **Squad:** Wildlife
- **Squishdate:** October 25, 2020
- **Collector number:** #633

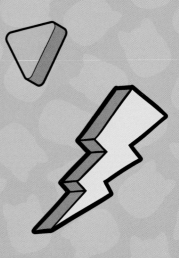

Bobbleheads and sneakers are two things that **CHET** the iguana loves to collect. He has almost 100 figurines, and a crazy story for almost every pair of sneakers—just wait until you hear about his latest pair!

CHIP

 Squad: Wildlife

 Squishdate: July 17, 2019

Collector number: #272

CHIP is a smart beaver! He is very kind and likes to help people. When he grows up, **CHIP** wants to be an aircraft designer and fly the jets that he creates.

CINNAMON

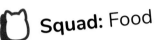 **Squad:** Food

Squishdate: November 20, 2020

Collector number: #692

CINNAMON and her best friend, **CARMELITA**, are like two peas in a pod, but sweeter! You can usually find them working on new stories, or at the mall—they love to window-shop. If you see this frozen yogurt out and about, she's sure to give you a big hug.

CLARA

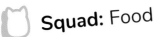

- **Squad:** Food
- **Squishdate:** March 10, 2020
- **Collector number:** #425

Have you ever seen a 'Mallow deadlift or power clean? It's time you met **CLARA**! This ice-cream sundae loves to see her friends at the local gym. They call themselves the "Sugar Box Gang."

COLE

- **Squad:** Sealife
- **Squishdate:** January 8, 2021
- **Collector number:** #813

Ready for some robot rumble fun? **COLE** is your guy if you like building things and tearing them down. This turtle loves making crazy cool robots, and letting them race and duel it out—just don't destroy his best bot!

CONNOR

- 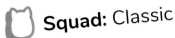 **Squad:** Classic
- **Squishdate:** April 17, 2020
- **Collector number:** #10

Mooove out of the way, **CONNOR** is racing you to the finish line! This cow is quite the athlete—you can catch him riding his bike everywhere! Where's the coolest place he's ever traveled? Cowlifornia!

CONRAD

- **Squad:** Food
- **Squishdate:** January 9, 2021
- **Collector number:** #815

Have questions about eating better? **CONRAD** is the corn for you! He wants to be a chef one day and loves food science. He knows that there is more to food than just taste, and wants to share more about the science behind it.

CRUZ

- **Squad:** Space
- **Squishdate:** December 22, 2020
- **Collector number:** #756

Mini-golf and guacamole are two things that **CRUZ** the sun can't live without, he'd play mini-golf every day if he could! He likes guac on everything, from breakfast and sandwiches to his mom's healthy avocado cupcakes!

DAJA

- **Squad:** Seasonal
- **Squishdate:** July 8, 2019
- **Collector number:** #265

Beaches, volleyball, and soaking up the sun are three of **DAJA**'s favorite things. This dolphin is the go-to gal for activities when the squad needs some fun in the sun!

DALTON

- **Squad:** Fantasy
- **Squishdate:** March 10, 2020
- **Collector number:** #422

DALTON adds chocolate milk to his marshmallow cereal, and hot sauce on his omelets. This scaly dragon has trouble sharing, and he needs you to help him learn how.

DANIELLE

- **Squad:** Seasonal
- **Squishdate:** July 14, 2020
- **Collector number:** #475

Meet **DANIELLE**. She loves playing music, video games, and drinking strawberry and kiwi smoothies. This bulldog is learning the piano and how to play the music from her favorite video games for her next recital. What song would you like to request?

DANNY

Squad: Classic

Squishdate: November 6, 2017

Collector number: #59

You will always want **DANNY** on your team! Why? He's the king of games! This dinosaur loves strategizing for board games, puzzles, outdoor sports, or scavenger hunts with his buddies.

DARYL

Squad: Space

Squishdate: July 9, 2020

Collector number: #484

Ready for liftoff? **DARYL** and **BROCK** are best buds and they're headed to the space station for an adventure. Their mission? To see the universe! **DARYL** the astronaut hopes to meet an alien or two, while **BROCK** wants to throw a football around the moon. Are you ready to go?

DASH

- **Squad:** Food
- **Squishdate:** November 29, 2020
- **Collector number:** #721

Meet **DASH**, the most artistic dumpling you'll find! **DASH** is inspired by classical works of art, and loves to create designs of his own. He dreams of appearing in a museum one day—would you like to see some of his work?

DAVINA

- **Squad:** Fantasy
- **Squishdate:** November 20, 2020
- **Collector number:** #693

Though she's really shy at first, octocorn **DAVINA** is a lot of fun. She does really great impressions and can almost always make you laugh. She wants to be a voiceover artist when she grows up, and has many voices and impressions that she just can't wait to try out.

DAWN

- **Squad:** Classic
- **Squishdate:** March 11, 2019
- **Collector number:** #195

Fawn **DAWN** is always up for a camping adventure. She is fluent in all animal languages, and loves to teach her friends about the different animals who live in the forest. She hopes to be a park ranger one day!

DELILAH

- **Squad:** Fantasy
- **Squishdate:** July 8, 2019
- **Collector number:** #263

Dinosaur **DELILAH**'s favorite season is fall—she loves baking anything with apple! Apple donuts, apple muffins, and especially caramel apples. Are you ready to become her baking assistant?

DELITA

Squad: Food

Squishdate: April 6, 2021

Collector number: #898

Meet **DELITA**! This dragon fruit is a morning person who enjoys crossword puzzles and breakfast! She makes a special granola almost every day. One day, **DELITA** wants to have her very own granola shop.

DENISE

Squad: Fantasy

Squishdate: March 12, 2019

Collector number: #197

DENISE loves donuts, iced coffee, and spending time with her family. She is the go-to mermaid for the latest hair and makeup trends in all the oceans, and still has time to keep her friends looking fab! You can recognize her by her signature nails and matching purple hair.

DEXTER

Squad: Fantasy

Squishdate: September 1, 2018

Collector number: #135

Dragon **DEXTER** is a unique individual who loves to fly around town. His dream is to become a pilot and travel the world, but for now **DEXTER** sticks to soaring the skies around his neighborhood showing off the tricks that his friend **BRODY** taught their group of fun-loving flying friends!

DREW

Squad: Fantasy

Squishdate: June 13, 2019

Collector number: #242

DREW is a confident little dragon who has a passion for baseball! When he's not playing in the Fantasy League, he likes to go on magical adventures to new stadiums. His creative mind loves learning new languages, and he hopes to one day become an airplane engineer so he can travel to all the enchanted stadiums!

DUKE
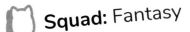

- **Squad:** Fantasy
- **Squishdate:** November 5, 2019
- **Collector number:** #365

Dragons **DUKE** and his brother **DOMINIC** are both fascinated by the ocean! **DUKE** pretends that he's a deep-sea diver, and wishes he could swim down to see the creatures who live at the bottom of the ocean.

DULCE

- **Squad:** Food
- **Squishdate:** April 9, 2021
- **Collector number:** #904

DULCE works part time as a gift-wrapper and makes the most beautiful bows. Even though the holidays can get stressful, she is dedicated to her work. Sweet **DULCE** is saving up to move across the world, one city at a time. If you need help wrapping a present, you know who to call!

DUSTIN

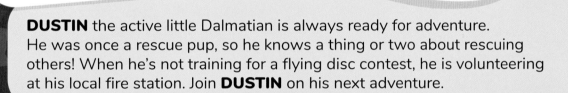

- **Squad:** Buddy
- **Squishdate:** July 8, 2020
- **Collector number:** #481

DUSTIN the active little Dalmatian is always ready for adventure. He was once a rescue pup, so he knows a thing or two about rescuing others! When he's not training for a flying disc contest, he is volunteering at his local fire station. Join **DUSTIN** on his next adventure.

EDIE

- **Squad:** Seasonal
- **Squishdate:** November 1, 2020
- **Collector number:** #645

Have you heard the weekly weather report? Make sure you tune in to **EDIE**'s *Eggcellent Weather Report* to find out! Easter-egg **EDIE** loves to talk about the weather, and always tries to dress the part. Her favorite ensemble is a jumpsuit with lightning bolts that glow in the dark!

EDWARD

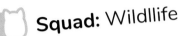

- **Squad:** Wildllife
- **Squishdate:** September 5, 2019
- **Collector number:** #306

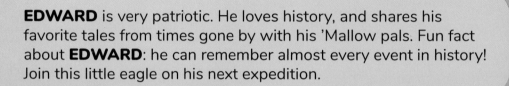

EDWARD is very patriotic. He loves history, and shares his favorite tales from times gone by with his 'Mallow pals. Fun fact about EDWARD: he can remember almost every event in history! Join this little eagle on his next expedition.

EMANGA

- **Squad:** Fantasy
- **Squishdate:** November 13, 2019
- **Collector number:** #373

Who loves cheese, space, and nature walks? EMANGA does! You can find this leopard with a grilled cheese in hand, gazing up at the stars and learning about constellations. She wants to build rocket ships when she grows up. Do you want to explore space with EMANGA?

EMILY

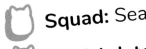 **Squad:** Seasonal

Squishdate: February 19, 2020

Collector number: #184-2

Spooky bat **EMILY** loves space! Her dream is to become an astronomer, and help name the new planets and stars that are discovered. **EMILY** also enjoys studying astrology. In her free time, she uses her telescope to study star patterns, and creates horoscopes for her friends.

FINN

Squad: Space

Squishdate: October 19, 2020

Collector number: #626

All aboard! **FINN** the conductor is collecting tickets—are you ready for an adventure? Alien **FINN** loves trains, and has a basement full of elaborate train tracks. When he's not building tracks or collecting tickets, you can find him reading more about his current planet and beyond.

FIONA

 Squad: Fantasy

 Squishdate: March 11, 2020

 Collector number: #428

Winter fairy **FIONA** lives in an ice castle in the North Pole near her wintry squad friends. She has an ice-cream shop, and can make any flavor you want. Don't forget to ask for her famous icicle sprinkles!

Fries

FLOYD

 Squad: Food

 Squishdate: March 24, 2020

 Collector number: #449

Have you ever met a French fry that loved adventure? Meet **FLOYD**! He dreams of leaving the kitchen for adventures he's only heard about! Climbing a mountain, sailing the sea, or even visiting the potato state, Idaho, to meet his family!

FREDDIE

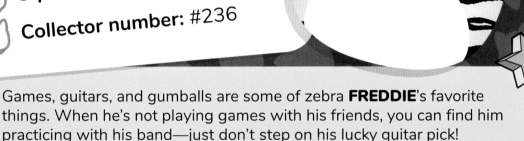

- **Squad:** Wildlife
- **Squishdate:** May 16, 2019
- **Collector number:** #236

Games, guitars, and gumballs are some of zebra **FREDDIE**'s favorite things. When he's not playing games with his friends, you can find him practicing with his band—just don't step on his lucky guitar pick!

GABBY

- **Squad:** Fantasy
- **Squishdate:** March 12, 2019
- **Collector number:** #199

Watch out for **GABBY**! Her favorite color is silver, but don't let that fool you, this figure-skating yeti is going for gold someday! When she's not on the ice, you can find her spending time with her friends and family.

GARY

- 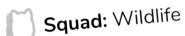 **Squad:** Wildlife
- **Squishdate:** December 1, 2017
- **Collector number:** #78

Nothing can stop giraffe **GARY** from reaching the finish line! You can't miss his long legs on the track, as he aspires to become a future Olympian. Want to know the best parts about **GARY**? He's fast on his feet, and can solve any problem that comes his way!

GIGI

- **Squad:** Buddy
- **Squishdate:** September 29, 2020
- **Collector number:** #597

This cuddly cat moves a mile a minute thanks to her favorite fuel— apple juice! When **GIGI**'s around, you're sure to smell a hint of apple before you see her. How much is too much? The sky's the limit!

GLADY

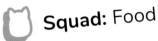

- **Squad:** Food
- **Squishdate:** July 12, 2021
- **Collector number:** #1120

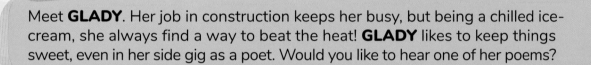

Meet **GLADY**. Her job in construction keeps her busy, but being a chilled ice-cream, she always find a way to beat the heat! **GLADY** likes to keep things sweet, even in her side gig as a poet. Would you like to hear one of her poems?

GLENA

- **Squad:** Food
- **Squishdate:** April 20, 2021
- **Collector number:** #971

GLENA is a water baby, and loves all kinds of water activities. Whether it's scuba diving, snorkeling, or surfing, you can always find this eggplant near the beach. Currently, **GLENA** is working hard and saving up to buy their first sailboat. Sailing lessons, here we come!

GORDON

- **Squad:** Sealife
- **Squishdate:** October 22, 2018
- **Collector number:** #163

You don't have to fear, **GORDON** is one of the friendliest 'Mallows around! This shark loves helping others so much, that one day he wants to start his own nonprofit charity!

GRACIA

- **Squad:** Wildlife
- **Squishdate:** June 7, 2021
- **Collector number:** #1040

Meet **GRACIA**. This 'Mallow loves all forms of dance, especially ballet, and dreams of being lead in her favorite ballet. She loves the feeling she gets when she steps onto the stage, and how the music helps her move. Will you bring her a bouquet for her next performance?

GRANT

- **Squad:** Wildlife
- **Squishdate:** September 24, 2019
- **Collector number:** #323

This gutsy goat has one dream—to become a soccer player! **GRANT** plays soccer with his friends at the park, at school, and at home with his friends. After they win, he celebrates with his favorite treat, a chocolate swirl ice-cream cone.

GREGORY

- **Squad:** Classic
- **Squishdate:** November 7, 2019
- **Collector number:** #369

Meet goat **GREGORY**, the go-to photographer for all things nature. **GREGORY** takes amazing photos all over the world, and just got back from a trip in the mountains! He loves sharing the things he sees with other 'Mallows. Where should he go on his next photo adventure?

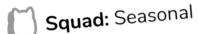

HANNA

- **Squad:** Seasonal
- **Squishdate:** August 7, 2019
- **Collector number:** #284

Have you met **HANNA**? This sweet hippo loves writing poetry, and every year writes a poem for each of her friends. Maybe one day you'll find a book of her poems in the 'Mallow Shop!

HARRISON

- **Squad:** Wildlife
- **Squishdate:** October 29, 2019
- **Collector number:** #357

HARRISON loves hockey, hiking, and horseback riding. He adores almost anything that involves being outdoors! Once a month, this hippo is a camp counselor for little 'Mallows, taking them on fun woodland hikes and camping trips.

HARRY

- **Squad:** Seasonal
- **Squishdate:** December 4, 2020
- **Collector number:** #734

HARRY loves to make music and wants to see the world—it's all he can think about! This horse started by reading poetry and writing down his feelings, and now he's going to school to write music. Maybe one day soon you'll hear one of **HARRY**'s songs.

HEATHER

- **Squad:** Wildlife
- **Squishdate:** September 6, 2020
- **Collector number:** #517

True to her species' ability to transform, dragonfly **HEATHER** is one of the mightiest 'Mallows around. No matter what obstacles come her way, she doesn't get discouraged. **HEATHER** is always able to solve and overcome any problems with positive solutions.

HENRY

- **Squad:** Sealife
- **Squishdate:** October 22, 2018
- **Collector number:** #168

Known by all the 'Mallows for his fantastic voice, turtle **HENRY** is a famous sports announcer. While he regularly provides commentary on basketball, football, and baseball games, his favorite sport is volleyball.

HOLLY

- **Squad:** Classic
- **Squishdate:** March 1, 2017
- **Collector number:** #4

Howdy, **HOLLY**! You can always find this friendly owl with a smile on her face, and a big hug waiting for you! She is incredibly outgoing, and can connect with everyone she meets.

HOOT

- **Squad:** Classic
- **Squishdate:** March 1, 2017
- **Collector number:** #3

HOOT and his sister **HOLLY** are complete opposites. He's quiet and likes to read in his tree fort with his friend **CAM**, but he's also a wonderful singer. This owl only sings when he thinks no one is listening—one day you might hear his hoot-iful voice!

HUGO

- **Squad:** Space
- **Squishdate:** January 23, 2021
- **Collector number:** #829

HUGO the planet loves adventure—he always seems to be on an imaginary quest! Whether it's from a new movie, a comic book, or hearing a story from a friend, **HUGO** takes bits of his regular day to create his own cool adventure and save the day!

HUMPHREY

- **Squad:** Buddy
- **Squishdate:** November 12, 2018
- **Collector number:** #174

HUMPHREY the hamster loves writing scripts and plays. When he's finished his latest work, he'll get together with all his 'Mallow friends and act it out! Join him, and see what role you'll land!

INDIE

- **Squad:** Sealife
- **Squishdate:** December 23, 2020
- **Collector number:** #760

Need a hand with some home improvements? **INDIE** is at your service! This hermit crab knows a thing or two about fixer-uppers, and is just a call away. You'll make **INDIE**'s day if you bring raspberry lemonade and freshly baked cookies!

IRVING

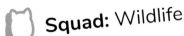

- **Squad:** Wildlife
- **Squishdate:** November 12, 2018
- **Collector number:** #171

Looking for adventure? Give rhino **IRVING** a call! He's always up for riding quad bikes, skydiving or even bungee jumping!

JACINDA

- **Squad:** Buddy
- **Squishdate:** November 21, 2020
- **Collector number:** #697

Flying disc and volleyball are two of poodle **JACINDA**'s favorite sports, especially at the beach. She loves to spend the day playing with friends. Whenever she wants to cool off, **JACINDA** just throws the disc towards the water and jumps in after it!

JACKIE

- **Squad:** Nature
- **Squishdate:** November 19, 2020
- **Collector number:** #685

JACKIE and her tulip sisters love to shop vintage. Whenever they travel together, they go on a retro hunt. Last month, they found hot-pink fuzzy phones that light up when you call. What will they bring home next?

JAELYN

- **Squad:** Sealife
- **Squishdate:** November 14, 2020
- **Collector number:** #665

Do you have anything to throw **JAELYN**'s way? This axolotl is practicing for a juggling contest! **JAELYN** loves to juggle and participates in competitions all over the place. This spring, they won first place for juggling 17 candy bars!

JAIME

- **Squad:** Fantasy
- **Squishdate:** May 5, 2021
- **Collector number:** #185-2

Sugar, spice, and everything in between can be found in pegasus **JAIME**'s home. She loves to bake goodies for her friends, and delivers weekly snacks to the 'Mallows in her squad.

JARIN

- **Squad:** Sealife
- **Squishdate:** June 17, 2019
- **Collector number:** #240

Have you ever seen a jellyfish juggle? **JARIN** may be the first! With dreams of joining the circus one day, **JARIN** practices his juggling skills with anything he can find.

JASON

- **Squad:** Buddy
- **Squishdate:** May 19, 2021
- **Collector number:** #368-2

Early mornings are hard for **JASON**, especially when he was up late studying! This donkey is learning to become a truck driver—he wants to drive trucks up through the mountains and beyond. **JASON** grew up loving trucks and can't wait to drive, but only after he's had his coffee.

JAYDA

- **Squad:** Sealife
- **Squishdate:** September 24, 2019
- **Collector number:** #322

JAYDA is a medical student who has a passion for helping others. She's also an expert at needlework. When she's not studying for exams, she's sketching designs and sewing costumes for her friends. What would you ask jellyfish **JAYDA** to sew for you?

JEANNE

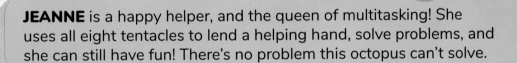

- **Squad:** Sealife
- **Squishdate:** September 10, 2019
- **Collector number:** #313

JEANNE is a happy helper, and the queen of multitasking! She uses all eight tentacles to lend a helping hand, solve problems, and she can still have fun! There's no problem this octopus can't solve.

JOANNE

- **Squad:** Sealife
- **Squishdate:** October 22, 2019
- **Collector number:** #159

Otter **JOANNE** is a faithful companion to mermaids on all types of adventures—they've even given her the nickname "sea pup"! She has a sweet tooth, and her go-to treat is honey buns. Emerald green is her favorite color.

JONNY

- **Squad:** Sealife
- **Squishdate:** September 10, 2020
- **Collector number:** #537

Have you seen **JONNY**? This fast-paced octopus is always busy and on the move! Even though he has eight tentacles, **JONNY** jokes that he could do with eight more. One thing to know about **JONNY**—he'll always speak up for what he believes in.

KAI

- **Squad:** Sealife
- **Squishdate:** October 22, 2018
- **Collector number:** #161

Orca **KAI** is the king of the sea! When he's not ruling the ocean, you can find him searching for sunken treasure. **KAI** is also a lover of art, and shows his creativity by making elaborate underwater sandcastles with his friends.

KAYCE

- Squad: Fantasy
- Squishdate: August 9, 2019
- Collector number: #286

Have you ever seen a panda pegacorn do Muay Thai? Meet **KAYCE**! She coaches soccer and trains in Muay Thai during the week. On the weekends, she attends tournaments and cheers on her team.

KEANU

- Squad: Fantasy
- Squishdate: January 5, 2021
- Collector number: #782

Kickball and dodgeball are two of camo dragon **KEANU**'s favorite games to play at recess. Whenever it's his turn to kick, he pretends that he's kicking the ball all the way into space. He hasn't kicked it that far yet, but maybe one day he will!

KEELY

Squad: Wildlife

Squishdate: May 13, 2019

Collector number: #227

Kangaroo **KEELY** is a soon-to-be-mommy, and blogger, who wants to start her own painting business. She paints murals for her friends and family, and dreams of one day painting a mural for her favorite place to visit, the opera house!

KEINA

Squad: Food

Squishdate: April 20, 2021

Collector number: #970

Never in one place for too long, sushi **KEINA** is a nomad. She loves to explore new places, speak new languages, and make new friends. **KEINA** can stay awake all night talking about all the amazing places to visit. Pack your bags if you're ready for a road trip with her!

116

KENDLA

- **Squad:** Food
- **Squishdate:** April 15, 2021
- **Collector number:** #949

Pumpkin spice latte **KENDLA** loves everything about being cozy. Whether it's sitting in front of the fireplace with a good book, or knitting a sweater for her friend **BERNICE**, you can always unwind with **KENDLA**. Her favorite season is fall—what season do you love most?

KENDRA

- **Squad:** Fantasy
- **Squishdate:** September 14, 2020
- **Collector number:** #550

Meet **KENDRA**. She loves to play sports, make new friends, and go on crazy adventures—one day she wants to travel or coach her own team! One of fox **KENDRA**'s favorite things about summer is going to camp, and last year she met two new 'Mallows who go to her school.

KENNY

- **Squad:** Fantasy
- **Squishdate:** April 23, 2019
- **Collector number:** #218

KENNY is not your average dragon—he loves watching movies, going dancing, and learning about the world of finance! When he's not on the dance floor, or catching the latest movie, he's studying for his master's degree.

KHALED

- **Squad:** Wildlife
- **Squishdate:** April 15, 2021
- **Collector number:** #937

You know you're in awe of cobra **KHALED**'s sparkly, smooth appearance! **KHALED** is one laid-back 'Mallow, and would spend all day basking in the sun if he could. Say hello and he just might invite you to fly a disc in the park, or go for a dip in the pool.

KIRK

 **Squad:** Wildlife

 **Squishdate:** March 1, 2018

 **Collector number:** #88

 You won't meet anyone as lovable as koala **KIRK**! His passion for learning and mentorship makes him the perfect fit for becoming a teacher. What will your first lesson with **KIRK** be?

KYA

 **Squad:** Fantasy

Squishdate: January 29, 2021

Collector number: #430-2

Strawberry cupcakes and blueberry smoothies are two of **KYA**'s favorite things. This koala has quite a sweet tooth, and loves all desserts, especially ones with berries—berry cakes, cookies, she even adds frozen berries to her hot cocoa! Fun fact about **KYA**: she's an expert tree-climber, even in the snow.

KYLA

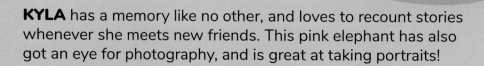

Squad: Seasonal

Squishdate: July 1, 2018

Collector number: #116

KYLA has a memory like no other, and loves to recount stories whenever she meets new friends. This pink elephant has also got an eye for photography, and is great at taking portraits!

LEANNE

Squad: Fantasy

Squishdate: July 8, 2020

Collector number: #480

Meet **LEANNE**. This unicorn loves spending time outside, especially with her family. **LEANNE** comes from a huge family of unipals, and enjoys having pizza Fridays—she always eats the biggest slice! Join her next pizza night.

LEELAND

- **Squad:** Food
- **Squishdate:** November 19, 2020
- **Collector number:** #688

Looking for a 'Mallow who will always have your back? It's time you met **LEELAND**! This lime is a team player both on and off the court, especially when it involves his sister **LETICIA**. Even though she's older than him and they don't always get along, he has her back.

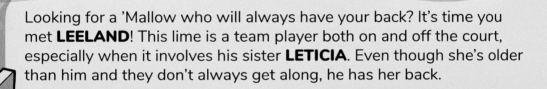

LEGACY

- **Squad:** Fantasy
- **Squishdate:** September 16, 2020
- **Collector number:** #564

Meet bunnycorn **LEGACY**. She has a beautiful butterfly garden, which is perfect for frolicking among the flowers and keeping an eye out for new butterflies. **LEGACY**'s favorite pastime is lying in the grass and reading a book.

LEN

- **Squad:** Seasonal
- **Squishdate:** January 27, 2021
- **Collector number:** #833

If ghost encounters and mysteries of the night are your thing, Franken bear **LEN** is the one for you! He loves to hear all about the unexplained, and creates his own theories on what is really going on. **LEN** wants to travel the world to find out more about what goes bump in the night. Do you want to join him?

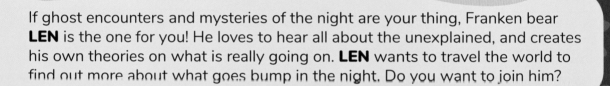

LENORA

- **Squad:** Wildlife
- **Squishdate:** October 10, 2019
- **Collector number:** #347

Have you ever met a water bird who couldn't sing? Loon **LENORA** can't! She comes from a family of beautiful singers, but she has a hard time joining in. **LENORA** wants to start a rock band so she can still sing in a unique way—will you join her band?

LEONARD

- **Squad:** Classic
- **Squishdate:** October 17, 2019
- **Collector number:** #351

Have you ever met a lion who didn't eat meat? Meet **LEONARD**—he's a vegetarian! He loves lentils, lasagna, and learning how to code. **LEONARD** enjoys naps like his older brother **RICHARD**, and is helping to create their website—the lion brothers!

LETICIA

- **Squad:** Food
- **Squishdate:** November 19, 2020
- **Collector number:** #687

Though they have very different personalities, lemon **LETICIA** and her brother, **LEELAND**, play tennis as one on the court. **LETICIA** is shyer than her brother, but once she's got her racket, the game is on. Watch out for her forehand!

LILOU

- **Squad:** Sealife
- **Squishdate:** December 23, 2020
- **Collector number:** #765

Dodgeball and needlepoint are two things that keep **LILOU** calm. This seal likes to focus and get creative when she's working on a new design. She even created personalized embroidery for everyone on her dodgeball team!

LOGAN

- **Squad:** Seasonal
- **Squishdate:** March 11, 2019
- **Collector number:** #194

If you want someone to keep you safe, **LOGAN** is your 'Mallow! He takes his job very seriously—**LOGAN** is one of Santa's helpers! He helps protect the North Pole, making sure that none of Santa's secrets get out. His favorite drink is hot cocoa with peppermint.

LUCILLE

Squad: Sealife

Squishdate: October 22, 2018

Collector number: #162

LUCILLE loves living near the water! This seal always finds new creatures, hidden gems, and her favorite—rocks—whenever she goes on a dive. Ask her to show you her amazing rock collection!

LUDWIG

Squad: Wildlife

Squishdate: October 30, 2020

Collector number: #641

Log cabins and snowboarding are two of **LUDWIG**'s favorite things— he loves the great outdoors. This frog runs a ski lodge that sits at the top of a hill, so every morning when he wakes up, he can see snow-covered trees for miles around. Join him for a sunrise cruise down the slopes.

LUNA

- **Squad:** Seasonal
- **Squishdate:** April 3, 2019
- **Collector number:** #77-2

The cold can't stop **LUNA**'s dancing feet. She brings the heat with her smooth moves. Looking for a penguin 'Mallow to lift you up when you're down? **LUNA** is your girl!

MAGGIE

- **Squad:** Sealife
- **Squishdate:** May 22, 2019
- **Collector number:** #239

MAGGIE is no ordinary stingray—she's a stingray with a degree! She just received her physician assistant master's and can't wait to start helping people. This busy stingray loves cooking, volleyball, and, of course, watching hospital dramas in her spare time.

MALCOLM

- **Squad:** Classic
- **Squishdate:** November 19, 2020
- **Collector number:** #684

Have you ever met a soccer-playing mushroom? **MALCOLM** is the one for you! He's the goalie on his team. They've won the championship three years in a row!

MANNY

- **Squad:** Seasonal
- **Squishdate:** November 17, 2017
- **Collector number:** #74

MANNY the snowman is quite the handyman. He enjoys picking up the pieces. He's known for building the most memorable gingerbread houses every year, and hopes to connect creativity and machines as an engineer in the future.

MARIO

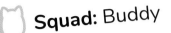 Squad: Buddy

Squishdate: July 10, 2019

Collector number: #266

Have you met **MARIO** the German shepherd? His parents want him to be an architect, but he wants to be a pastry chef, and bake tall, elaborate cakes. **MARIO** has always loved building things, so he can't wait to make things out of cake! What kind of cake should he bake first?

MARITZA

Squad: Nature

Squishdate: October 12, 2020

Collector number: #619

MARITZA has her sights set on equality for all squads. From the Sealife to Fantasy squads, this cactus knows that all 'Mallows are equal. She wants to focus on treating 'Mallows fairly when they move to a new place, especially if they're part of a new squad.

MATEO

- **Squad:** Buddy
- **Squishdate:** July 10, 2019
- **Collector number:** #267

MATEO gives the best hugs! This Rottweiler is known for spreading smiles wherever he goes. **MATEO** doesn't know what he wants to be when he grows up, but he does know that he wants to help people.

MATT

- **Squad:** Sealife
- **Squishdate:** October 22, 2018
- **Collector number:** #156

Did you see those crazy tee-shirt designs? Yes, **MATT** the seal helped inspire them! He loves graphic design and fashion, and dreams of being a fashion designer one day.

MAUI

- **Squad:** Food
- **Squishdate:** September 27, 2019
- **Collector number:** #329

Skateboards and scuba diving are two scary things that pineapple **MAUI** is determined to conquer her fear of. She already checked roller coasters and Rollerblading off her list. **MAUI** doesn't like to be scared, so she tries to beat her fears by trying new things. Can she help you overcome one of your fears?

MAURICE

- **Squad:** Wildlife
- **Squishdate:** October 10, 2019
- **Collector number:** #343

MAURICE the moose *loves* chocolate-chip pancakes, and eats them almost every Saturday. His dad makes a giant stack for **MAURICE** and his sisters to share. One day, **MAURICE** wants to host a pancake show so he can try all kinds of pancakes.

MAX

Squad: Fantasy

Squishdate: September 26, 2020

Collector number: #593

Meet **MAX** the techie! This raccoon loves technology. When he isn't playing video games or learning about cars, he enjoys rocking out to his favorite band.

MAXWELL

Squad: Seasonal

Squishdate: July 1, 2017

Collector number: #25

MAXWELL is a little reserved, but he's a real sweetie at heart! He's a poet, and has written some great stories, too. If you're lucky, he'll share them with you.

MAYA

- **Squad:** Food
- **Squishdate:** March 24, 2020
- **Collector number:** #454

Fresh and cool, with a hint of sweet—that's how all the 'Mallows describe **MAYA**. This kind ice cream is the best one to know if you need a helping hand. She'll give you a little tough love, but always knows the right things to say to turn your frown upside down.

MEDINA

- **Squad:** Food
- **Squishdate:** April 6, 2021
- **Collector number:** #897

Did you catch that flash of yellow? It's **MEDINA** on her longboard! This super-fast slushie works at a coffee shop, and sometimes helps with the deliveries. She's an expert at juggling coffee orders.

MILA

- Squad: Classic
- Squishdate: April 17, 2017
- Collector number: #17

Elephant **MILA** is making moves! She has found her healthy fix through creative recipe tips, which she uses to treat her friends and family! Are you ready to get happy and healthy with **MILA**?

MILES

- Squad: Fantasy
- Squishdate: July 8, 2019
- Collector number: #258

Meet **MILES**, the computer guru. This dragon loves to learn about the technological world around him. When he's not behind a screen, he enjoys building robots with his friends. **MILES** aspires to be an engineer one day.

MILO

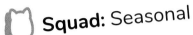

- **Squad:** Seasonal
- **Squishdate:** December 10, 2018
- **Collector number:** #178

MILO the mummy is the master of languages, and speaks ten fluently! His favorite pastime is studying extinct languages and teaching them to his friends. He dreams of becoming a linguist for the 'Mallow Museum so he can combine his love of languages and history!

MISTY

- **Squad:** Buddy
- **Squishdate:** May 14, 2019
- **Collector number:** #232

If you want to take a ride on the wild side, **MISTY** the mischievous mouse is the gal for you. **MISTY** is not your typical mouse— though she is tiny, she is mighty. She loves hockey, baseball, car races, and horses! She'd love to ride professionally one day.

MO

Squad: Food

Squishdate: November 21, 2020

Collector number: #696

Hop in the car and buckle up! **MO** is going to take you on an adventure. This sushi is a tour guide and loves to drive others around to show off the hidden gems in the neighborhood.

MURRAY

Squad: Seasonal

Squishdate: April 11, 2021

Collector number: #908

Have you met **MURRAY**? This mouse dreams of being a master chef and is a bit of a mischief-maker. When **MURRAY** isn't assisting **GINA** or making his famous meat platters, he's probably starting snowball fights with his cousin, **MISTY**.

MYRTLE

- **Squad:** Seasonal
- **Squishdate:** February 20, 2020
- **Collector number:** #399

Frankenstein **MYRTLE** likes pumpkin-spice sorbet and caramel-apple ice cream—she loves when fall flavors hit the store! When she was just a mini-monster, **MYRTLE** wanted to be a hairdresser. Now she owns her own salon! Be sure to stop in for a special 'Mallow monster 'do.

NATHAN

- **Squad:** Buddy
- **Squishdate:** May 13, 2019
- **Collector number:** #221

Who loves oranges and tacos and is ready to keep you company? **NATHAN**! This homebody cat is always ready to curl up for a movie, or have an adventure in the latest video game, so long as there are tacos nearby!

NEBULA

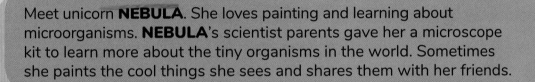

- **Squad:** Fantasy
- **Squishdate:** June 22, 2020
- **Collector number:** #472

Meet unicorn **NEBULA**. She loves painting and learning about microorganisms. **NEBULA**'s scientist parents gave her a microscope kit to learn more about the tiny organisms in the world. Sometimes she paints the cool things she sees and shares them with her friends.

NITRO

- **Squad:** Sealife
- **Squishdate:** May 14, 2021
- **Collector number:** #1011

Meet **NITRO**. This hammerhead shark loves to tell stories, and wants to be a director one day. He's most excited about filming documentaries, bringing awareness to stories that people might not know about. Give him a camera and watch him go!

NIXIE

- **Squad:** Seasonal
- **Squishdate:** January 21, 2021
- **Collector number:** #504-2

It's almost Halloween, and time for **HOLLY**'s famous costume contest! In the spirit of friendly competition, butterfly **NIXIE** has big hopes for first place. She's dressing up as a skeleton, do you think she will win?

OCTAVIA

- **Squad:** Sealife
- **Squishdate:** June 1, 2020
- **Collector number:** #463

Meet **OCTAVIA**. This octopus has a helpful pep in her step, just like her sister **JEANNE**! **OCTAVIA** loves to paint nails, and wants to open a mobile nail salon. She doesn't know where to start, though—will you help her?

OLGA

- **Squad:** Sealife
- **Squishdate:** November 17, 2020
- **Collector number:** #678

Are you looking for a trivia partner? **OLGA** is a history buff like you wouldn't believe. She comes from a family of octopus librarians, who taught her new historical facts every day. Can **OLGA** join your squad?

OPAL

- **Squad:** Fantasy
- **Squishdate:** June 5, 2020
- **Collector number:** #466

Meet **OPAL**—she's the only girl in a family with four older octopus brothers who love her dearly. Last year they gave her a sparkly pink dirt bike! She especially loves to ride after the rain so she can splash around in the really big puddles.

ORIN

- **Squad:** Food
- **Squishdate:** September 27, 2019
- **Collector number:** #332

ORIN is a silly orange—he responds to questions with more questions, and on Fridays he tries to do everything backward! Thankfully, his friends like his silliness and play along with his jokes.

PACO

- **Squad:** Wildlife
- **Squishdate:** August 9, 2019
- **Collector number:** #285

PACO is quite the entertainer among his friends. He loves to be up to date on current events, and adores sports. This parrot's favorite sport is soccer, and he hopes to become a sports broadcaster when he grows up.

PEP

- **Squad:** Food
- **Squishdate:** April 23, 2021
- **Collector number:** #998

Meet **PEP**. He's a delivery driver who loves to sing while he's working. Pizza **PEP** loves blasting music so he can sing and dance along his route. Next time you see him, give him a wave.

PERRY

- **Squad:** Sealife
- **Squishdate:** October 22, 2018
- **Collector number:** #155

Hang 10 with dolphin **PERRY** for the day and you're sure to become an avid surfer! When he's not surfing, you can find him relaxing near the beach, enjoying frozen yogurt, and waxing his board for the next wave.

PHILLIPPE

- **Squad:** Seasonal
- **Squishdate:** July 1, 2017
- **Collector number:** #28

PHILLIPPE enjoys a good game of hopscotch with his friends, especially **MARCO**. This frog enjoys taking pictures of his family and friends, which he'll be doing this Valentine's Day. Join him!

PHYLLIS

- **Squad:** Food
- **Squishdate:** September 27, 2019
- **Collector number:** #335

Have you met **PHYLLIS**? She's captain of the swim team, and can't wait to get back in the pool. If she could, this peach would turn into a mermaid!

PILAR

- **Squad:** Wildlife
- **Squishdate:** December 23, 2020
- **Collector number:** #764

Ready for a relaxing afternoon with grasshopper **PILAR**? Lace up your shoes and off you go! **PILAR** likes to start off with a little sport followed by a snack. What do you want to do first?

PIPER

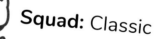

- **Squad:** Classic
- **Squishdate:** March 17, 2017
- **Collector number:** #8

Ready for super **PIPER**? You will never see this penguin without a paintbrush in her hand! She is quite artistic, constantly creating new paintings in her art class. She loves to draw portraits and make friendship bracelets with her buddies.

PONDEROSA

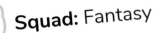

- **Squad:** Fantasy
- **Squishdate:** July 2, 2019
- **Collector number:** #257

Have you ever met a seafaring unicorn? Now you have! **PONDEROSA** flies ahead of her ship to watch for land, bad weather, and scout for danger. In her downtime, she enjoys root-beer floats, and sharing stories with the crew.

PRINCE

- **Squad:** Buddy
- **Squishdate:** March 1, 2018
- **Collector number:** #95

PRINCE is considered royalty in the playground. You can't miss this pug doing flips and tricks across the monkey bars with his adventurous 'Mallow pals. Want to join in the fun?

PRISCILLA

- **Squad:** Wildlife
- **Squishdate:** August 16, 2019
- **Collector number:** #292

Have you met **PRISCILLA**? This perky peacock is always ready to lend a helping hand—there's not much she can't do! **PRISCILLA** loves to spend time with her friends, and finds many new activities for them to try.

PUFF

- **Squad:** Classic
- **Squishdate:** March 17, 2017
- **Collector number:** #7

PUFF loves extra marshmallows in his cocoa, and sharing smiles with his friends. He can be a bit silly sometimes, but this penguin is great at keeping secrets.

RAHIMA

 Squad: Wildlife

 Squishdate: June 3, 2021

 Collector number: #1036

You've probably never met a 'Mallow as strong as **RAHIMA**. She's training for the biggest competition around, where she hopes to compete in the weightlifting category. Even though her muscles might intimidate you, she's as sweet as she is strong.

RAISY

 Squad: Food

 Squishdate: April 23, 2021

 Collector number: #999

Meet **RAISY**. Last week, this ramen dozed off and had a crazy dream—she dreamed that she discovered a new galaxy, and that 'Mallows could fly around in space! She flew off into the stars, and then she woke up. One day, maybe it can come true!

RAMONA

- **Squad:** Seasonal
- **Squishdate:** July 2, 2019
- **Collector number:** #251

Meet **RAMONA**, the hopscotch queen! This red panda loves milkshakes (of every flavor), and wants to be a bus driver like her dad when she grows up.

REGINALD

- **Squad:** Buddy
- **Squishdate:** March 1, 2018
- **Collector number:** #97

Captain of the lacrosse team, corgi **REGINALD** is a fearless leader. He loves to spend time with his teammates, on and off the field—especially when it involves watching one of his favorite movies.

REINA

- 🐱 **Squad:** Wildlife
- 🐱 **Squishdate:** July 17, 2019
- 🐱 **Collector number:** #271

Meet **REINA**. This fabulous butterfly loves fashion, fun, and drawing. Her love for fashion inspires many of her beautiful creations. She is outgoing and adores spending time with friends. Maybe one day you'll see her artwork on the cover of a magazine!

RENNE

- 🐱 **Squad:** Food
- 🐱 **Squishdate:** March 28, 2021
- 🐱 **Collector number:** #876

RENNE is one fun 'Mallow. This little latte loves calligraphy, drawing, and playing lacrosse! Her favorite colors are purple and blue, and she loves a good movie night. What can **RENNE** draw for you?

RESSIE

- **Squad:** Food
- **Squishdate:** April 22, 2021
- **Collector number:** #988

Meet red apple **RESSIE**. She spends most of her time reading books. From ancient history to chemistry, she just loves to learn! Recently, **RESSIE** read a book about dinosaurs, and now she likes to look for fossils at the beach. What's your favorite kind of book to read?

REY

- **Squad:** Seasonal
- **Squishdate:** July 14, 2020
- **Collector number:** #490

Meet **REY**. This shy shark has an eye for fashion, fun, and capturing "the perfect moment" for all of his friends. **REY** loves to take pictures, and add funky filters before sending the photos to his friends. One day he will have a gallery full of colorful snapshots to explore!

RIAH

- **Squad:** Fantasy
- **Squishdate:** November 2, 2019
- **Collector number:** #360

Have you met **RIAH**? This little yeti is like a ray of sunshine— she makes 'Mallows smile wherever she goes! **RIAH** is kind, considerate, and loves to give hugs to all her friends and family. Her favorite food is peaches, and she's great at tae kwon do.

RICKY

- **Squad:** Sealife
- **Squishdate:** October 22, 2018
- **Collector number:** #158

Living up to his clownfish species, **RICKY** knows how to make all the other 'Mallows laugh! Catch him at his next open mic night and see for yourself!

ROCKY

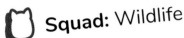

- **Squad:** Wildlife
- **Squishdate:** December 1, 2017
- **Collector number:** #79

Don't stop racoon **ROCKY**—he's on a roll! **ROCKY** has been an adventure seeker since he was little, and plans on climbing his first summit this year. Grab your hiking boots and bring the fun!

ROMAN

- **Squad:** Space
- **Squishdate:** December 21, 2020
- **Collector number:** #755

Need some help making the right decision? **ROMAN** is here to help! **ROMAN** wants to be a leader when they grow up and knows that it's important to take care of the world we live in. This planet likes to play fair, eat clean, stay green, and think about others.

RONNIE

- **Squad:** Wildlife
- **Squishdate:** September 19, 2020
- **Collector number:** #581

RONNIE loves building birdhouses—last week he made a purple two-story birdhouse with green shutters. His sister **BELANA** helps him paint them and makes sure they are ready to move into. Do you want to buy a birdhouse from **RONNIE** the cow?

ROSIE

- **Squad:** Classic
- **Squishdate:** September 19, 2019
- **Collector number:** #318

Meet **ROSIE**. She's visiting her family from the other side of the pond! Rosie loves crunchy biscuits, going to concerts with her friends, and spending time with her nanna. Her nanna makes the best tea, and always has yummy treats ready when **ROSIE** the pig comes over.

RUBY

- **Squad:** Seasonal
- **Squishdate:** November 17, 2017
- **Collector number:** #73

RUBY enjoys long walks on the ice with an occasional hot cocoa beverage. Reindeer **RUBY** is the North Pole's Christmas coordinator. She plans all the reindeer events leading up to the grand finale on Christmas Day.

RUDY

- **Squad:** Space
- **Squishdate:** December 20, 2020
- **Collector number:** #753

Ready for takeoff with **RUDY** the rocket? He and his best friend **DAXXON** are explorers on a mission to defend the universe, or so they tell their friends. They share a love for adventure and being helpful. Would you like to join them?

RUTABAGA

- **Squad:** Wildlife
- **Squishdate:** November 17, 2020
- **Collector number:** #677

Have you ever met a caterpillar who can't live without chocolate? Peanut butter cups and chocolate chip cookies are two of **RUTABAGA**'s favorite treats. And if you're making cookies, **RUTABAGA** has just one rule to follow—always add more chocolate chips!

SABRINA

- **Squad:** Fantasy
- **Squishdate:** May 14, 2019
- **Collector number:** #235

SABRINA is one of a kind! This caticorn has traveled the globe and seen amazing things. She wants to travel to every single country, and will even send you a postcard!

154

SAM

- Squad: Classic
- Squishdate: April 17, 2017
- Collector number: #19

SAM is the friend for you, but only if you can keep up! This dog is a runner and can race circles around his friends at the park. **SAM** absolutely loves the outdoors, and is always on the move.

SAMIR

- Squad: Sealife
- Squishdate: April 13, 2021
- Collector number: #919

Who's that 'Mallow leading the pack? It's **SAMIR**! This wonderful whale never planned on being in charge, but his kindness and consideration have helped him become an excellent leader. If you need some advice on making the best choice, give **SAMIR** a call!

SANTINO

- **Squad:** Wildlife
- **Squishdate:** November 12, 2019
- **Collector number:** #372

SANTINO makes the best blueberry pancakes, his dad taught him how to add the blueberries just right. When he's not making pancakes for all his friends, you can find **SANTINO** playing soccer—he wants to be a professional goalie someday.

SAWYER

- **Squad:** Wildlife
- **Squishdate:** March 1, 2018
- **Collector number:** #90

Find a penny, pick it up, and all day long you'll have good luck! Squirrel **SAWYER** loves to collect pennies, beads, and shiny knickknacks that he finds in the forest during the day. Join him on a treasure-hunting expedition!

SCARLET

- **Squad:** Food
- **Squishdate:** September 27, 2019
- **Collector number:** #336

Meet **SCARLET**. This sweet strawberry loves all things theater and dance—she wants to be a costume designer and a performer on Broadway. Her father taught her how to sew, and every year she makes the costumes for her school plays. One day her dad will be front row for one of her shows!

SCOUT

- **Squad:** Fantasy
- **Squishdate:** August 2, 2017
- **Collector number:** #48

SCOUT loves to paint, but this panda gets a bit messy. By the end of the day, all the colors get on his white fur, so he looks like a painting himself!

SCRAPPER

- **Squad:** Seasonal
- **Squishdate:** February 20, 2020
- **Collector number:** #407

SCRAPPER is known as a daredevil—he creates the fireworks and lightshow for the Skeleton Squad and rides a motorcycle onstage. This butterfly also makes a mean devil's food cake, and bakes one for the band at the start of every tour.

SERENE

- **Squad:** Fantasy
- **Squishdate:** February 25, 2021
- **Collector number:** #853

Here's **SERENE**, the calmest squirrel you'll meet! Just like her name, she's cool, collected, and the perfect 'Mallow to help you take a deep breath. She meditates every day, and loves to give her friends advice.

SEVDA

- **Squad:** Food
- **Squishdate:** April 20, 2021
- **Collector number:** #969

Follow **SEVDA** to the ice! She dreams of becoming a world-class skater and is almost always at the rink, perfecting her routine. This boba tea loves to help others learn her sport, so grab your skates and take a whirl!

SHANNON

- **Squad:** Food
- **Squishdate:** October 14, 2020
- **Collector number:** #625

Order up! Ice cream **SHANNON** is a barista who loves to have fun at work, and specializes in moody drinks. She'll ask how your day is going, and if you want to order from the regular menu or if you would prefer a moody drink. What kind of drink are you in the mood for?

SHAUNA

- **Squad:** Sealife
- **Squishdate:** January 8, 2021
- **Collector number:** #793

SHAUNA and her friend **LANDON** rule the stage. They've been dubbed the king and queen of karaoke among their friends. Shell **SHAUNA** is a crowd-pleaser and warms up the crowd with a new ballad every week. Can you guess her next song?

SHAY

- **Squad:** Sealife
- **Squishdate:** December 29, 2020
- **Collector number:** #768

Need a workout pal at the gym? **SHAY** has limbs and jokes to go around! Lifting weights, reading plays, and a good joke are squid **SHAY**'s way of life. He loves to recite his favorite monologues with some added humor for his friends.

SHELDON

- **Squad:** Sealife
- **Squishdate:** October 10, 2019
- **Collector number:** #346

Seahorse **SHELDON** enjoys spending time by himself and learning more about the ocean he lives in. He loves learning about all the plants, other sea creatures, and making friends with the people he meets along the way. Fun fact about **SHELDON**: he wants to be a jellyfish when he grows up!

SHENA

- **Squad:** Fantasy
- **Squishdate:** November 3, 2020
- **Collector number:** #648

SHENA is looking for someone to play catch with, so grab a glove! She's working on her curveball because she wants to try out for the softball team this spring. Though she's great at batting, this dog wants to become the best pitcher around. Will you help her?

SIMON

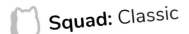

- **Squad:** Classic
- **Squishdate:** March 17, 2017
- **Collector number:** #9

Want a buddy to just relax with? Sloth **SIMON** is your perfect match. If you can't find him, he's probably at the store buying another video game! He is the greatest video gamer on the block. Fun fact about **SIMON**: he loves virtual reality. If it were up to him, he would teleport himself in a second!

SIMONE

- **Squad:** Sealife
- **Squishdate:** October 27, 2020
- **Collector number:** #634

Grab your opera glasses and get ready for a musical journey, shrimp **SIMONE** is about to go onstage! **SIMONE** is an opera singer with a magical voice. You're always in for a treat if you can catch her while she's in town.

SINCLAIR

- 🐾 **Squad:** Food
- 🐾 **Squishdate:** November 18, 2020
- 🐾 **Collector number:** #682

Avo-toast **SINCLAIR** and his cousin **AUSTIN** love to talk about outer space, but they always disagree on whether aliens exist. **AUSTIN** thinks they do, but **SINCLAIR** needs more proof. He wants to join **AUSTIN** on a space adventure to find out. Are you ready for liftoff?

SKYLER

- 🐾 **Squad:** Wildlife
- 🐾 **Squishdate:** May 13, 2019
- 🐾 **Collector number:** #229

Skunk **SKYLER** is obsessed with gardening—he helps his grandmother, and has developed quite the green thumb! He may give you a fright when you first meet him, but this skunk is a softie at heart.

SOPHIE

- **Squad:** Wildlife
- **Squishdate:** August 2, 2017
- **Collector number:** #46

Inspired by the flowers near her home, sheep **SOPHIE** is an aspiring fashion designer. She loves creating new looks and staging fashion shows with her friends.

STACY

- **Squad:** Sealife
- **Squishdate:** August 28, 2019
- **Collector number:** #299

STACY is a shy squid—she prefers to be home with her friends or even by herself. Big groups of 'Mallows make her a little nervous, so she loves to learn and explore through books. She's quiet at first, but all her friends know that she can be very silly.

STANLEY

- Squad: Costume
- Squishdate: December 23, 2020
- Collector number: #20-2

Need a friend who will support and protect you? Well, then you've got a friend in **STANLEY**. This panda has been practicing karate since he was small. He even has his black belt test next month! When he's not kicking a punching bag, he is writing poetry.

STARLA

- Squad: Sealife
- Squishdate: June 15, 2020
- Collector number: #471

Meet seahorse **STARLA**. She loves iced tea, board games, and exploring. She's an ocean studies major, and wants to keep the ocean clean and safe for everyone. **STARLA**'s parents taught her to care about environmental issues and to keep the planet safe for all creatures.

SYDNEE

- **Squad:** Fantasy
- **Squishdate:** September 5, 2020
- **Collector number:** #511

Meet **SYDNEE**. This squirrel wants to be a superspy when she grows up! She loves to watch spy and undercover-agent movies with her dad—they even have their own secret code words. **SYDNEE** wants her dad to build her a super-secret treehouse, would you like to help?

TALLY

- **Squad:** Seasonal
- **Squishdate:** January 18, 2021
- **Collector number:** #89-4

TALLY can't wait for Halloween, this year she's wearing two costumes! While she's trick or treating, she's dressing up as a vampire cat, and for **HOLLY**'s party she's wearing her lucky witch hat.

TANK

- **Squad:** Sealife
- **Squishdate:** November 18, 2020
- **Collector number:** #679

Because of his size, **TANK** may look like a menacing 'Mallow, but he lives by the motto "peace, love, and minding my business." This hammerhead shark hippy wants to live in harmony and just enjoy life.

TASHA

- **Squad:** Wildlife
- **Squishdate:** December 9, 2019
- **Collector number:** #383

Zebra **TASHA** loves hot pink with sparkles, and goes bowling with her dad every weekend. She even has hot-pink shoes, and a sparkly bowling ball that matches! For good luck, she rubs the bottom of her shoes three times, and then blows a kiss while her ball rolls down the lane.

TATI

Squad: Fantasy

Squishdate: April 10, 2019

Collector number: #210

TATI loves dancing, baking, and exploring with her friends. This dragon wants to save the world one day at a time. Catch her with her friends out in the wild or in the library, reading up on her next big adventure!

TAVIO

Squad: Food

Squishdate: January 8, 2021

Collector number: #812

Tamale **TAVIO** loves magic tricks and scary movies. This year he wants to have a scary magic birthday party. He wants a hypnotist or a spooky magic show, and a giant magician hat piñata.

TERESA

Squad: Fantasy

Squishdate: April 10, 2019

Collector number: #211

Who loves the color purple, eating delicious food, and helping people? **TERESA**! This busy unicorn is studying to be a doctor by day and is a foodie by night.

TERRY

Squad: Wildlife

Squishdate: February 20, 2020

Collector number: #411

Gobble-gobble, it's time for turkey **TERRY**'s famous garlic mashed potatoes! Every year **TERRY** visits his old foster family to meet the current foster 'Mallows. He knows it's not always easy growing up that way, but he tries to show the mini 'Mallows that one day they'll be okay!

169

TEX

- **Squad:** Food
- **Squishdate:** March 24, 2020
- **Collector number:** #453

Cheese, onions, and a little extra spice are some of taco **TEX**'s favorite things. **TEX** is a chef and loves to use new ingredients to mix things up. This tasty taco knows how to throw a party, especially when his favorite toppings are in town!

TINA

- **Squad:** Wildlife
- **Squishdate:** December 1, 2017
- **Collector number:** #81

TINA's style is one for the books. Her patterned clothing isn't the only thing that stands out about this sassy 'Mallow. She is known for her unforgettable hairstyles, which leave every 'Mallow excited for their next hairdo!

TITO

- **Squad:** Wildlife
- **Squishdate:** August 9, 2019
- **Collector number:** #290

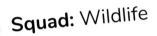

Toucan **TITO** is known for being quiet, but when he has something funny to say, all his friends crack up. **TITO** wants to be a counselor when he grows up to help kids who are quiet like him.

TODD

- **Squad:** Wildlife
- **Squishdate:** April 15, 2019
- **Collector number:** #214

Have you ever wondered how to play the harmonica? Chicken **TODD** is a harmonica hero—he can play almost any song he hears! Watch for him on the newest game show *Play That Tune* to see if he's the next big harmonica sensation!

TOMMY

- **Squad:** Buddy
- **Squishdate:** October 20, 2019
- **Collector number:** #352

Border collie **TOMMY** loves to play pool and card games. Someday he dreams of opening up an arcade! **TOMMY** wants to add his favorite food to the menu—loaded baked potatoes with cheese, sour cream, and extra bacon. Would you visit his arcade?

TRACEY

- **Squad:** Fantasy
- **Squishdate:** March 11, 2019
- **Collector number:** #191

3, 2, 1, GO! **TRACEY** spends her time racing cars and trucks, and one day wants to be a professional monster-truck driver! For her birthday this year, the zooming zebra wants to have a monster-truck-themed party.

TRINITY

- **Squad:** Fantasy
- **Squishdate:** December 10, 2019
- **Collector number:** #384

Meet triceratops **TRINITY**, she loves tapioca pudding, tortellini, and tamales. **TRINITY** likes baseball even more than her brother **TREY**, and wants to be a team manager when she grows up.

TRISTAN

- **Squad:** Prehistoric
- **Squishdate:** March 10, 2018
- **Collector number:** #172

Want to get in shape? Schedule a session with triceratops **TRISTAN**, an amazing personal trainer! He's training for a bodybuilding competition right now, and after that, a marathon!

TRUDY

- 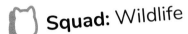 **Squad:** Wildlife
- **Squishdate:** October 22, 2018
- **Collector number:** #166

Ladybird **TRUDY** is always up on the latest trends, which is why her friends love it when she does their hair! When she's not in the salon, you can catch her reading a magazine, shopping, or enjoying a beautiful walk in the park.

TULA

- **Squad:** Fantasy
- **Squishdate:** January 6, 2021
- **Collector number:** #783

TULA loves rock climbing and reading, but not at the same time! She and her best friend **VANESSA** go climbing on the weekends. They have matching helmets and support each other as they climb. After a long day, this bear can't wait to curl up and read her latest book.

VERONICA

- **Squad:** Sealife
- **Squishdate:** October 22, 2018
- **Collector number:** #157

If you like adventure, pretzels, and crossing books off your reading list, **VERONICA** is the octopus for you! With a book or two in each tentacle, you can be sure she's on some amazing adventures.

VIOLET

- **Squad:** Sealife
- **Squishdate:** September 1, 2018
- **Collector number:** #139

Octopus **VIOLET** is the bright, spirited queen of the sea, who has a passion for adventure and exploration! She loves to join **KAI** on his quests for sunken treasure and uses her degree in archaeology to identify where the treasure originated!

WADE

- **Squad:** Seasonal
- **Squishdate:** February 20, 2020
- **Collector number:** #419

Werewolf **WADE** is a pretty big guy, and at first glance gives many 'Mallows a fright! He tries not to take it personally, but one day **WADE** hopes his looks won't make other 'Mallows so scared of him. Fun fact about **WADE**: he plays the violin.

WANDA

- **Squad:** Food
- **Squishdate:** September 27, 2019
- **Collector number:** #333

Watermelon **WANDA** loves all things strategy—chess, dominoes, and making the perfect sandwich. When she visits her grandparents, they take her to play games in the park, and afterwards, she makes them her famous sandwiches.

WENDY

- **Squad:** Classic
- **Squishdate:** March 17, 2017
- **Collector number:** #6

You can always find **WENDY** out on the basketball court (she won the Most Valuable Player award last year) or in the science lab, since chemistry is her favorite subject. This frog wants to be a famous scientist when she grows up, and likes to paint pictures of her experiments.

WESLEY

- **Squad:** Wildlife
- **Squishdate:** November 12, 2019
- **Collector number:** #371

WESLEY grew up with his aunt, and loves making paper airplanes. His aunt is a musician, and he gets to travel the world on her tours. Wombat **WESLEY** makes each of the band members a good-luck airplane to throw at the start of all their shows.

WILLY

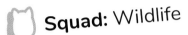

- **Squad:** Wildlife
- **Squishdate:** October 10, 2019
- **Collector number:** #342

WILLY was the runt of his litter—but that doesn't hold this wolf back! He is fascinated by storms and wants to be a weatherman when he grows up! He loves bow ties and has a weather-themed bow-tie collection that he can't wait to show off.

WINNIE

- **Squad:** Seasonal
- **Squishdate:** July 2, 2019
- **Collector number:** #256

WINNIE is not your ordinary walrus, she loves making ice-cream sundaes, and sandcastles (not at the same time). When she's not making her specialty gummy-bear sundae, you can find her creating her next sandcastle masterpiece!

XANDER

- **Squad:** Prehistoric
- **Squishdate:** September 17, 2020
- **Collector number:** #565

Roar! **XANDER**'s here! But don't be frightened, this lovable T. rex has a heart of gold! **XANDER** loves spending time with his friends and family. He wants to travel the world and find new adventures!

XANDRA

- **Squad:** Sealife
- **Squishdate:** September 11, 2020
- **Collector number:** #541

There's no 'Mallow more well-traveled than **XANDRA**! She used to be a professional scuba diver and visited over 50 countries before she hung up her snorkel to work in the city. Unlike her hermit neighbors, **XANDRA** is an outgoing and friendly crab, who loves to party with her best friend **CARLOS**.

XIMENA

- **Squad:** Food
- **Squishdate:** January 15, 2021
- **Collector number:** #824

Scrapbooking is how mango **XIMENA** likes to spend her time. She loves to celebrate her family by creating beautiful books for each of them. Last week she started one for her birthday, one of her favorite days ever. Do you want to scrapbook with **XIMENA**?

XIOMARA

- **Squad:** Wildlife
- **Squishdate:** October 22, 2020
- **Collector number:** #630

Grab your goggles and a notebook, it's time for class with **XIOMARA**! This black panther is a chemistry teacher and loves to have fun in her classes. Last week she made bath bombs and slime—what will she teach next?

YASMIN

- **Squad:** Fantasy
- **Squishdate:** December 29, 2020
- **Collector number:** #770

Hedgehog **YASMIN** has always enjoyed lending a helping hand—even as a mini 'Mallow she would offer to pass out the snacks in school. Now that she's older, she has started a club that volunteers every month. Do you want to join?

YOLLIE

- **Squad:** Fantasy
- **Squishdate:** March 11, 2020
- **Collector number:** #431

YOLLIE is the sweetest yeti around! This gal loves going to the cabin with her best friends **RIAH** and **GABBY**. She adores snow cones and making snowmallows in winter. Join Yollie on her next trip to the cabin!

YURI

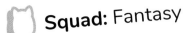

- [ ] **Squad:** Fantasy
- [ ] **Squishdate:** June 24, 2020
- [ ] **Collector number:** #474

Meet **YURI** the yeti. He loves plants and has a growing collection of indoor plants including a cactus named **FRED**. **YURI** lives in the city where there aren't a lot of trees, so he tries very hard to keep the plants alive and happy. What plant should **YURI** get next?

ZAC

- [ ] **Squad:** Seasonal
- [ ] **Squishdate:** December 10, 2018
- [ ] **Collector number:** #183

ZAC is a biology enthusiast with a brilliant mind. This zombie is a medical student who dreams of becoming a heart surgeon. When he's not studying for exams, **ZAC** likes to stay active and play flag football with his friends.

ZAYLEE

Squad: Fantasy

Squishdate: November 16, 2020

Collector number: #672

Zany Bigfoot **ZAYLEE** is here, are you ready for some fun? **ZAYLEE** loves to do silly things like walk sideways in the playground, and drink milkshakes through a crazy straw. What funny things should she do next?

ZEKE

Squad: Fantasy

Squishdate: September 19, 2019

Collector number: #316

Have you met zebra **ZEKE**? He's in charge of the pit crew that keeps **TRACEY**'s race car running smoothly. **ZEKE** loves noodles, nachos, and watching the cars he works on fly by on the racetrack.

Introducing ...

FIFI

the Red Fox

WOW! fact

Fifi helps her 'Mallow friends stay super chill by teaching them yoga.

SQUISHMALLOWS SUPERFAN QUIZ

Take this quiz to see how much you know about those quirky, snuggly, colorful SQUISHMALLOWS!

1 What was the original name of Squishmallows?

A. Squashed Mushems

B. Squishy Squooshems

C. Marvelous 'Mallows

2 This 'Mallow is a member of which squad?

A. Buddy

B. Sealife

C. Wildlife

3 Without checking, can you name this 'Mallow?

A. Leeland

B. Kenny

C. Leonard

4 What word would you associate with space-loving Daryl?

A. fruity

B. sporty

C. canine

?

5
Which of the following is not a Squishmallows squad?

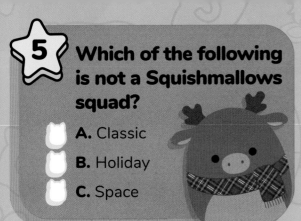

- **A.** Classic
- **B.** Holiday
- **C.** Space

6
What is the favorite color of Blanca, the rainbow kangaroo?

- **A.** white
- **B.** black
- **C.** rainbow

7
Which is the rarest category of Squishmallows?

- **A.** Select
- **B.** Ultra Rare
- **C.** Special Edition

8
How tall is the tallest 'Mallow to date?

- **A.** 16 inches
- **B.** 20 inches
- **C.** 24 inches

9
What sort of animal is root veggie Rutabaga?

- **A.** glow worm
- **B.** grasshopper
- **C.** caterpillar

10
In which year was Jack's squishdate?

- **A.** 2020
- **B.** 2021
- **C.** 2022

Now check the answers on page 192 and figure out your score.

1-3 correct answers
NOT QUITE A NEWBIE
You may not be the Squishmallows' MVF (Most Valuable Fan), but you're off and running with this performance! Spend some time getting to know the Squishmallows to earn a higher score next time.

4-7 correct answers
MEGA 'MALLOWS FAN!
Top quizzing—you're quite the contestant! Most of the 'Mallows you've met before, but there are still some in the squad who'd love to make your acquaintance. So why not give your collection a boost?

8-10 correct answers
#1 SQUISHMALLOWS SUPERFAN!
Huge congrats are due to you, superfan! You know almost all there is to know about our ultra-cuddly, collectible friends, the Squishmallows! If you were a 'Mallow, your rating would be Select!

MY 'MALLOW

MY WAY!

Ever wanted to design your own one-of-a-kind 'Mallow? Well, what are you waiting for? Grab some crayons or markers, then get creative!

Fill in the facts for your brand-new 'Mallow below.

Name:

_____

 Squad: ....

 Squishdate: ....

Now describe all the things that your 'Mallow loves best, and which friends it likes to hang with.

TOP TIP: Why not choose friends from the "Meet the 'Mallows!" pages?

MEET MY 'MALLOW!

....

....

....

....

Don't forget to customize your 'Mallow—try these accessories for inspo!

FAN FAVORITES

Beauty is in the eye of the collector, of course, but if you're stuck on which Squishmallows should join your squad next, here are **30 fan favorites** to consider—they're some of the squishiest, most adorable 'Mallows around!

Check off any 'Mallows that already belong to your squad, and decide on the ones you need next!

CAM
☐ got! ☐ need!

LOLA
☐ got! ☐ need!

FIFI
☐ got! ☐ need!

WINSTON
☐ got! ☐ need!

HANS
☐ got! ☐ need!

AVERY
☐ got! ☐ need!

LEONARD
☐ got! ☐ need!

ARCHIE
☐ got! ☐ need!

GORDON
☐ got! ☐ need!

WENDY
☐ got! ☐ need!

MAUI
got! need!

MALCOLM
got! need!

TATI
got! need!

SHELDON
got! need!

BENNY
got! need!

ROSIE
got! need!

FLOYD
Fries
got! need!

CARMELITA
got! need!

BROCK
got! need!

PRINCE
got! need!

SAMIR
got! need!

MAYA
got! need!

SINCLAIR
got! need!

JACK
got! need!

RUTABAGA
got! need!

BABS
got! need!

CHANEL
got! need!

ZEKE
got! need!

JEANNE
got! need!

PACO
got! need!

Pages 26—27
SQUISH CROSS!

```
    ¹F
     I
     F                    ²H
³P R I N ⁴C E             E
         L                D
       ⁵C A M             G
         S                E
         S                H
     ⁶W I N ⁷S T O N
         C      E         G
                A
             ⁸B L A C K
                I
          ⁹Z    F
       ¹⁰S E L E C T
          K
          E
```

Pages 186—187
SQUISHMALLOWS SUPERFAN QUIZ

1. B—Squishy Squooshems
2. B—Sealife
3. C—Leonard
4. C—canine
5. B—Holiday
6. B—black
7. A—Select
8. C—24 inches
9. C—caterpillar
10. A—2020